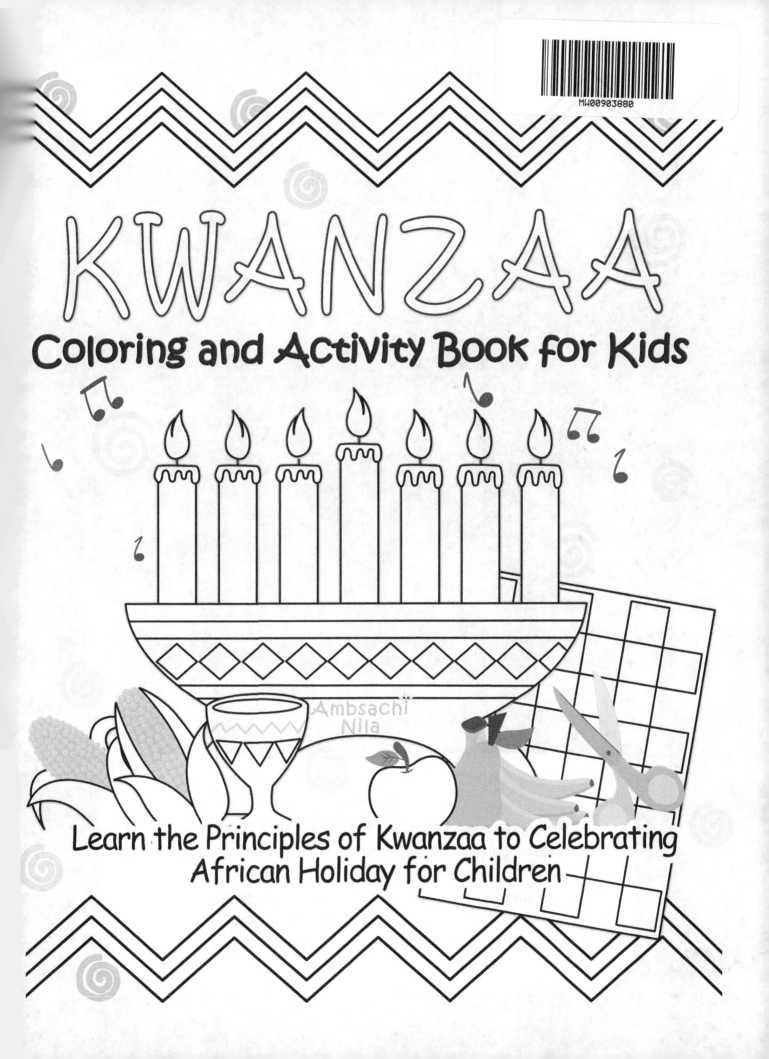

KWANZAA
Coloring and Activity Book for Kids

Learn the Principles of Kwanzaa to Celebrating
African Holiday for Children

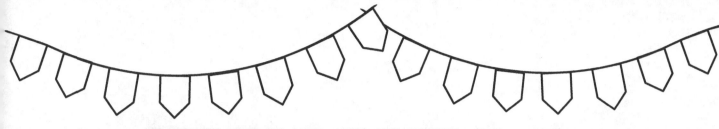

KWANZAA

is a very joyous holiday!
It is a celebration of all Africans and African-Americans.
Regardless of faith, all Africans can celebrate Kwanzaa.
And they do so!
The Kwanzaa holiday celebrates our family,
community, values, culture and history!

Find Africa and color it!

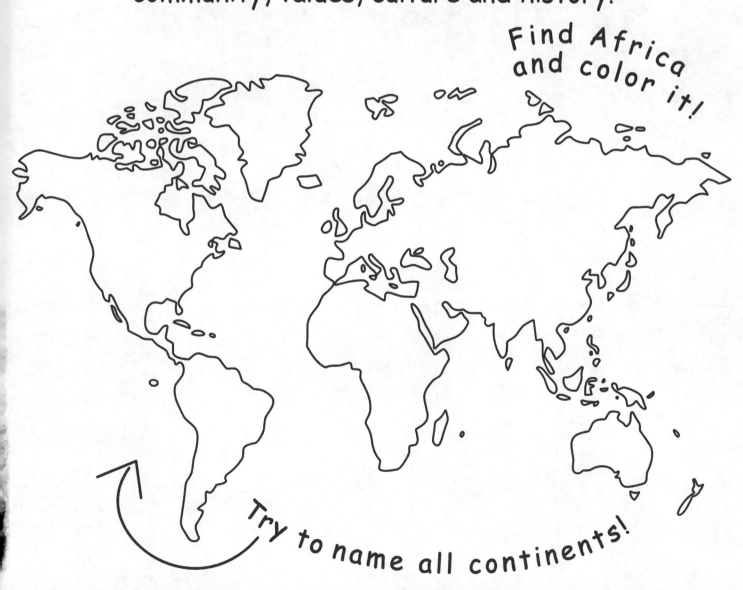

Try to name all continents!

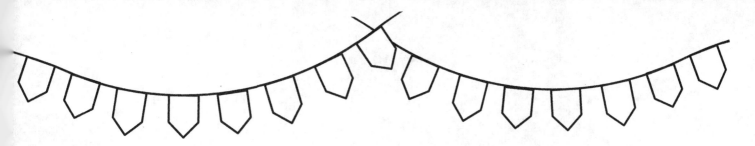

Kwanzaa was established in **1996** by Professor **Maulana Karenga**. It is celebrated every year from December 26 to January 1, so the celebrating lasts as long as **7 days**!

DECEMBER

THIS BOOK BELONGS TO:

○ ○ ○ ○ ○ ○ ○ ○ ○ ○ ○ ○ ○ ○ ○

TEST COLOR

Each day of the holiday we celebrate one of **The Seven Principles** of Kwanzaa which are:

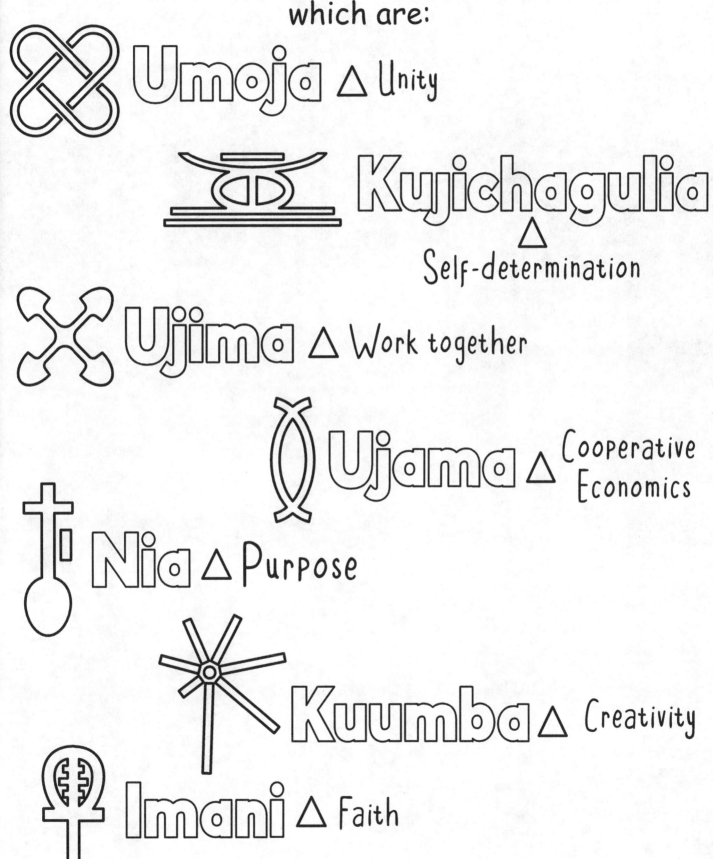

Umoja △ Unity

Kujichagulia △ Self-determination

Ujima △ Work together

Ujama △ Cooperative Economics

Nia △ Purpose

Kuumba △ Creativity

Imani △ Faith

Color them all!

The Seven Principles of Kwanzaa are called:

NGUZO SABA

Kwanzaa principles are written in Swahili,
an East African language. The word KWANZAA
also comes from this language and actually means:

FIRST FRUITS
OR
HARVEST TIME

It is the end of harvest time in Africa that are
the origins of this holiday.
We celebrate the harvest and give thanks for it.

Kwanzaa is a special holiday!
The celebration is accompanied by various symbols.
Let's get to know them!

(m-kay-kah)

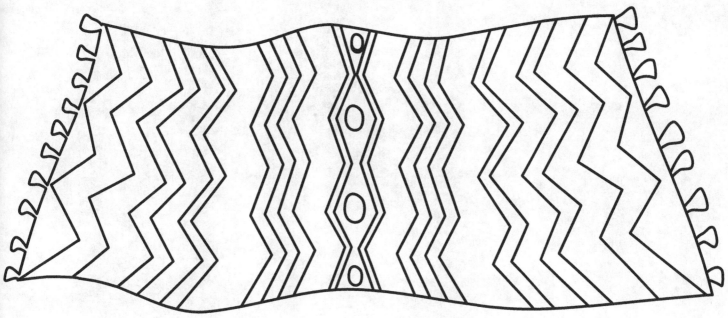

Mkeka is the Kwanzaa mat placed on the table.
It is a foundation of our tradition and history.
We are putting it on the table, on which we then place the Kinara
and the other Kwanzaa symbols.

KIKOMBE CHA UMOJA

(kee-KOM-bay chah oo-mo-jah)

It's the Kwanzaa
Unity Cup
that honoring
and thanking
our African ancestors.

MISHUMAA SABA

(mee-shoo-MAH-ah SAH-bah)

It is seven candles, each representing one principle of Kwanzaa.

KINARA

(kee-NAH-rah)

Kinara is a candlestick holder
made of wood.

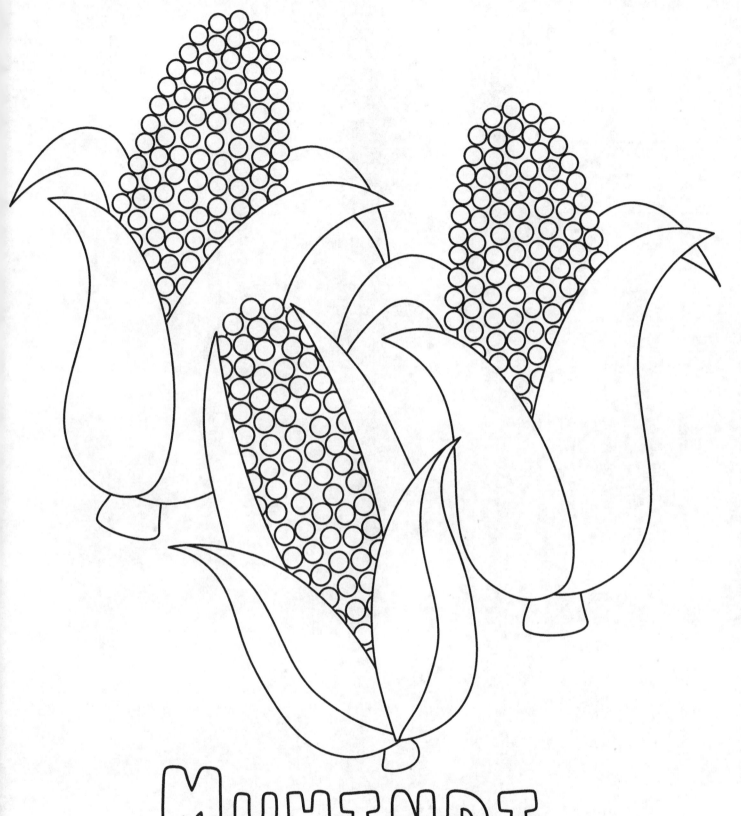

MUHINDI
(moo-HEEN-dee)

are ears of corn.
One ear of corn is given to each child in the family.

MAZAO

(Mah-ZAH-oh)   (The crops)

are fruits and vegetables symbolizing the African festival of the end of the harvest. This is the basis of Kwanzaa!

Try to name them all and then color them!

ZAWADI

(zah-WAH-dee)
are the gifts we give each other during Kwanzaa.

BENDERA

(bayn-day-rah)

The flag is a supplemental symbol. Color it according to the instructions to find out what each color represents:

1 - red
2 - black
3 - green

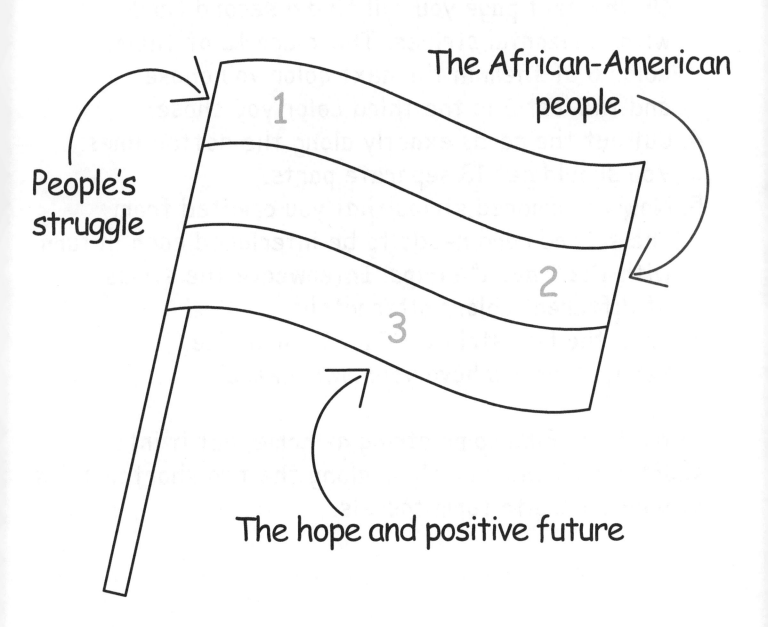

The African-American people

People's struggle

The hope and positive future

To create your mkeka follow these directions:

1. Choose the three colors you want for your mkeka.
2. Color the card next to it with the vertical stripes in one of the colors of your choice.
3. On the next page you will find a second card with horizontal stripes. There are 12 of them, color 6 of them in the next color you chose and the last 6 in the third color you chose.
4. Cut out the cards exactly along the dotted lines. You should get 13 separate parts.
5. Now the colored strips that you created from the second card needs to be interlaced each in turn with the "Part 1" strips. Interweave the strips of different colors alternately.
6. Tape the last strip to "Part 1" with glue.
7. Ready! Now you have your own mkeka!

Extra task: Find some string at home, cut it into short pieces and glue them along the two shorter sides of your mkeka to form tassels.

Let's design your own Mkeka!

Part 1

Let's design your own Mkeka!

1 DAY

UMOJA
(oo-MOH-ja)

is the principle of Kwanzaa,
which we celebrate on the first day.
It is a day of family and community unity.
On this day we light a black candle.

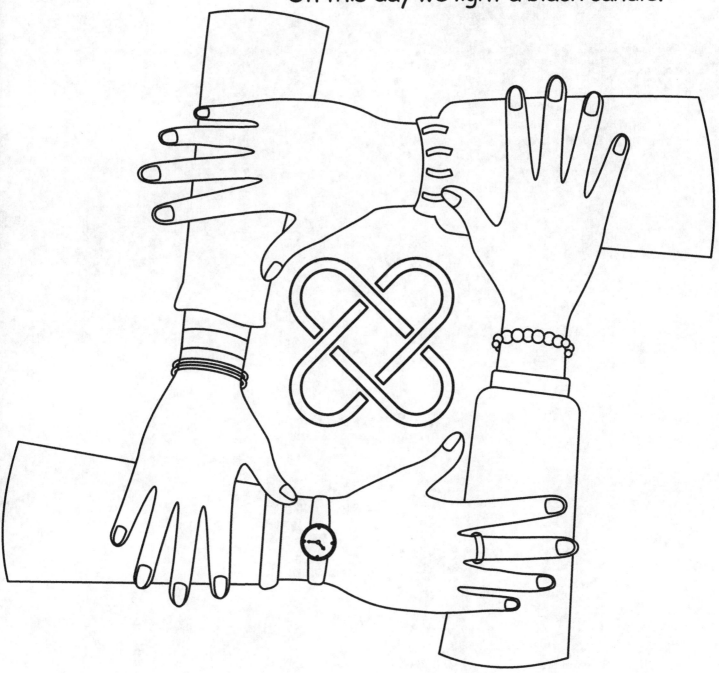

Count the items and connect them
a line with the correct answer.

Color them all!

Learn how to draw a kinara! Draw and color a kinara according to the template below in the designated boxes.

KUJICHAGULIA

(koo-jee-CHA-goo-lee-ah)

SELF-DETERMINATION

It's a principle that talks about deciding for ourselves,
who we want to be and what we want to do.
On this day we light the first red candle on the kinara.

Connect the elements with their shadows with a line.

Color them all!

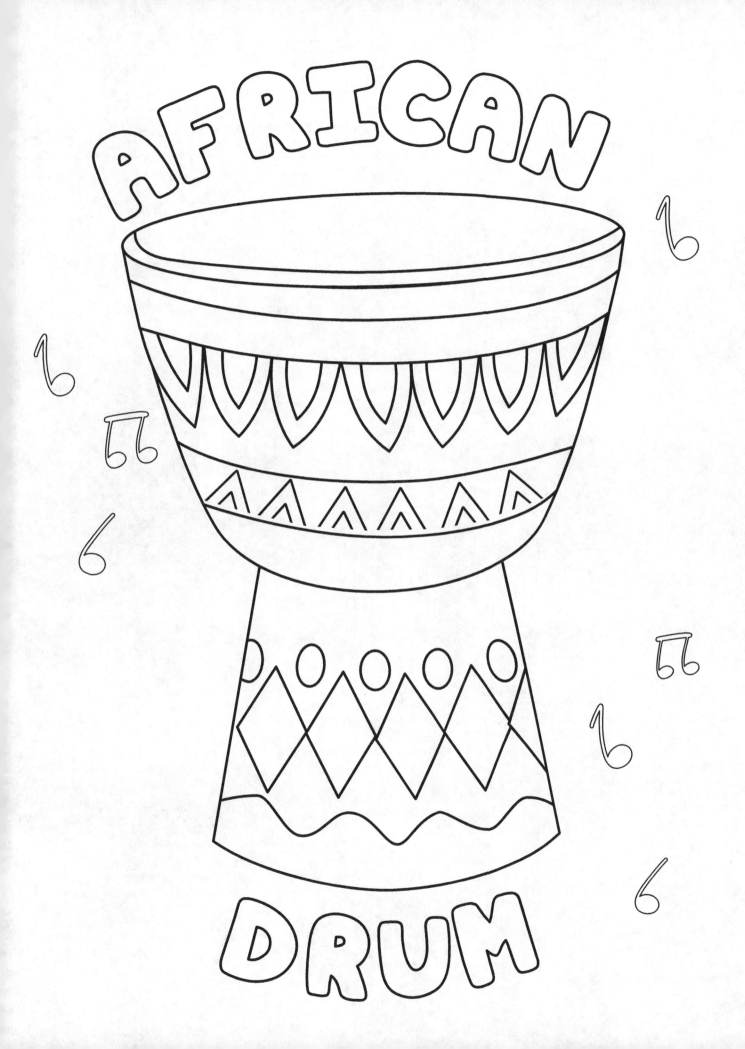

Find 9 words related to Kwanzaa.
Search words in directions: →, ↘, ↓

```
S E V E N F H O L A D R
W D K W A L I W R N T F
A X F W J B I H S G O A
H R T D A N C E V Q E M
I D S N K N Y C H L J I
L I C T M A Z A O D E L
I F V U F I S A M A S Y
J S R N A A E N A F U I
N R V I M B E R B R S O
T F Y T R A D I T I O N
E B S Y L N R B T C I E
W S O M Y P W A X A N F
```

- Kwanzaa
- Dance
- Seven
- Mazao
- Unity
- Africa
- Family
- Swahili
- Tradition

See the solution on the next page :)

```
S E V E N F H O L A D R
W D K W A L I W R N T F
A X F W J B I H S G O A
H R T D A N C E V Q E M
I D S N K N Y C H L J I
L I C T M A Z A O D E L
I F V U F I S A M A S Y
J S R N A A E N A F U I
N R V I M B E R B R S O
T F Y T R A D I T I O N
E B S Y L N R B T C I E
W S O M Y P W A X A N F
```

Let's solve the maze. Good luck!

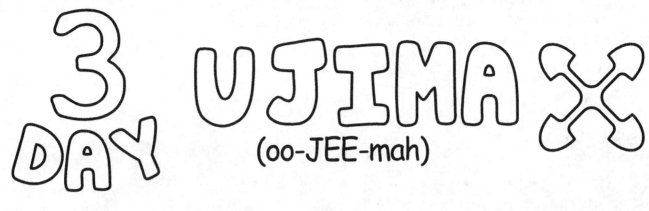

3 DAY UJIMA
(oo-JEE-mah)

WORKING TOGHETER AND RESPONSIBILTY

On the third day we light the first green candle.

Write the missing numbers:

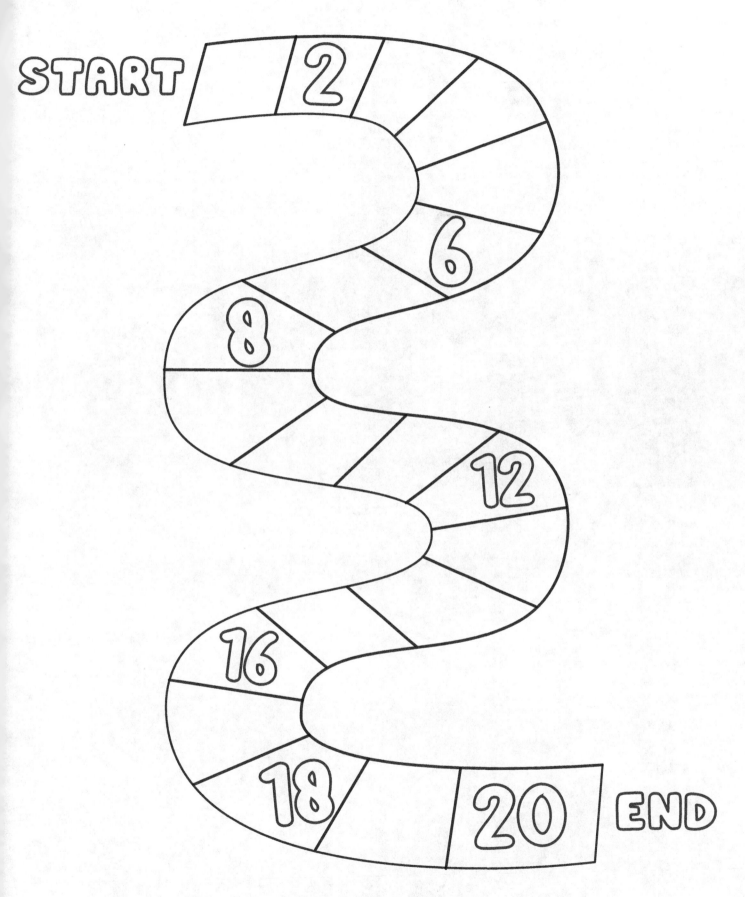

Color them all!

Find and pair the same characters.

Color them all!

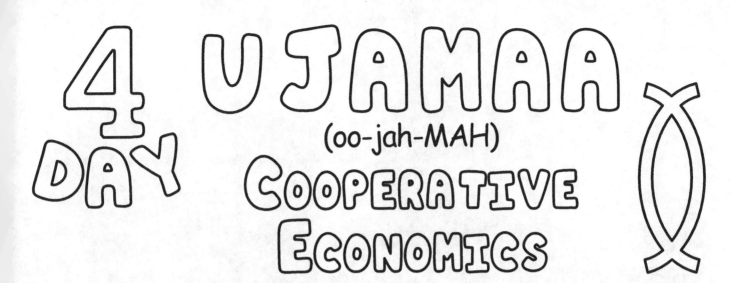

DAY 4 UJAMAA
(oo-jah-MAH)
COOPERATIVE ECONOMICS

The principle of the fourth day of kwanzaa means
supporting African-American businesses,
because we want them to grow and flourish.
That's why we use their services and buy products there.
On this day we light the second red candle on the kinara.

Count all the items and write the answer in the empty Circles at the bottom of the page.

Color them all!

Find 9 words related to Kwanzaa.
Search words in directions:

```
P V P U R P O S E H C Y
E C H W A L S I T A O T
R S R L V E R H S P R P
C E L E B R A T I O N R
S R E L A B R H T I O I
M I K T O T S A Z N E N
A P I A F I I R M E S C
L S N X T A N V T S U I
G R A P E S G E I S Q P
I F R J C I I S I T E L
E B A A L E N T T Y Y E
W S O M Y P G A X O N F
```

- Kinara	- Purpose	- Creativity
- Principle	- Grapes	- Corn
- Celebration	- Harvest	- Singing

See the solution on the next page :)

```
P V U R P O S E H C Y
E C H W A L S I T A O T
R S R L V E R H S P R P
C E L E B R A T I O N R
S R E L A B R H T I O I
M I K T O T S A Z N E N
A P I A F I I R M E S C
L S N X T A N V T S U I
G R A P E S G E I S Q P
I F R J C I I S I T E L
E B A A L E N T T Y Y E
W S O M Y P G A X O N F
```

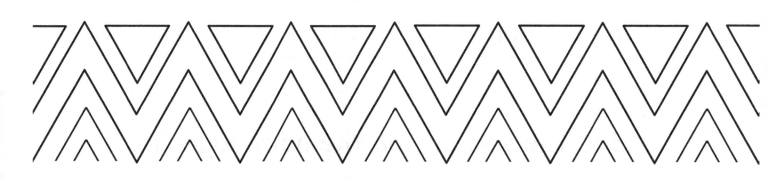

Which one is different?

Color them all!

NIA ✝
(NEE-ah)
PURPOSE

5 DAY

Kwanzaa's fifth principle is that each of us should care
about developing and building our community to make it great.
We remember our heroes and read books,
maybe one day we will become one of them!
On the fifth day we light the second green candle.

Learn how to draw the Unity Cup! Draw and color it according to the template below in the designated boxes.

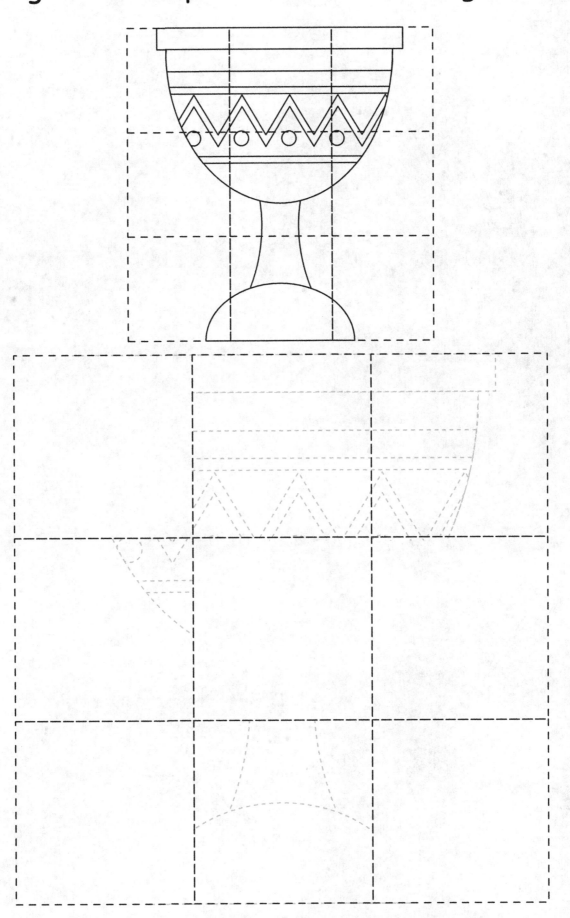

Let's solve the maze. Good luck!

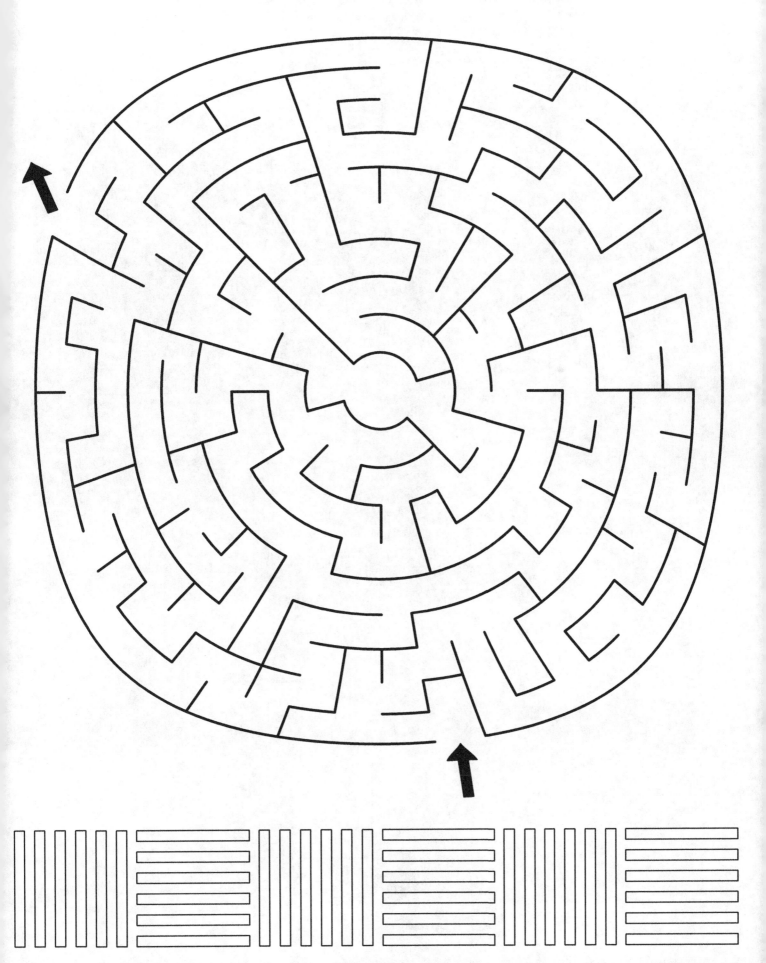

Connect the elements with their shadows with a line.

Color them all!

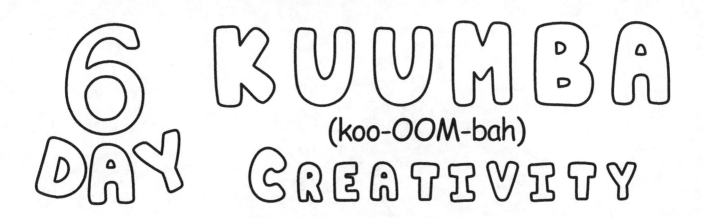

6 DAY KUUMBA

(koo-OOM-bah)

CREATIVITY

On the sixth day of the Kwanzaa celebration,
we are decorating our homes for Karamu!
We try to do our best to make our community m
ore beautiful than we found it.
On the sixth day we light the last red candle.

Write the missing letters in the blank spaces so that they form the correct word.

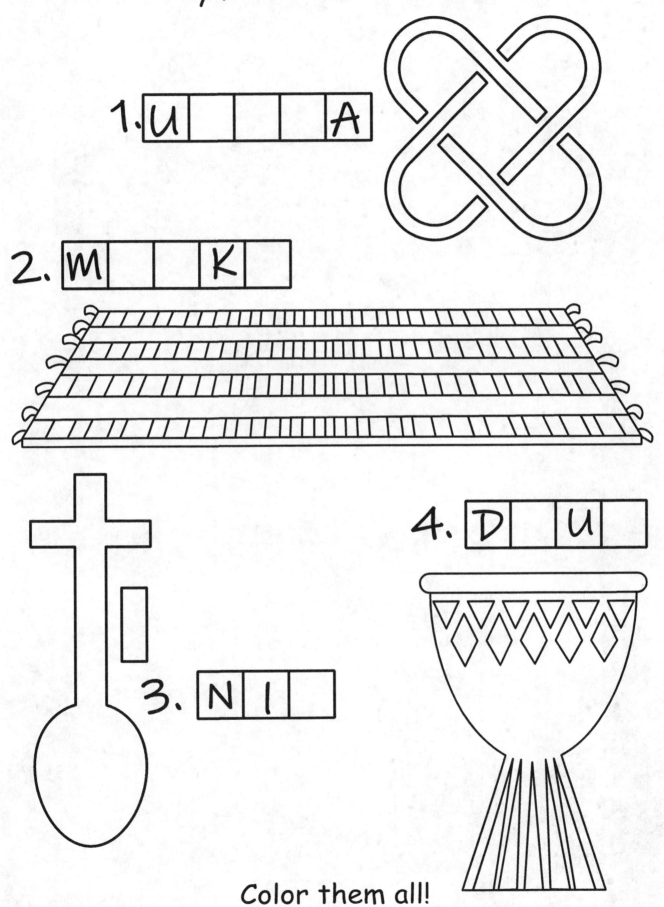

1. U [ ] [ ] A

2. M [ ] K [ ]

3. N I [ ]

4. D [ ] U [ ]

Color them all!

Find 9 words related to Kwanzaa.
Search words in directions:

```
A T A Y E R H O L H L Y
E F H K A L B W T D I M
R S Q N A T I O N J G U
F D T T V R H G E E A H
D R C O R Q A I R N S I
K U U M B A Y M Z T E N
A M V T F I O D U E S D
L S E P U M P K I N U I
A J B E N D E R A A Q N
I R Q V I N A C I S E J
E H I S T O R Y J Y I E
W D H A Y T E N F S N F
```

- Pumpkin	- Kuumba	- Karamu
- Drum	- Bendera	- History
- Unity	- Muhindi	- Nation

See the solution on the next page :)

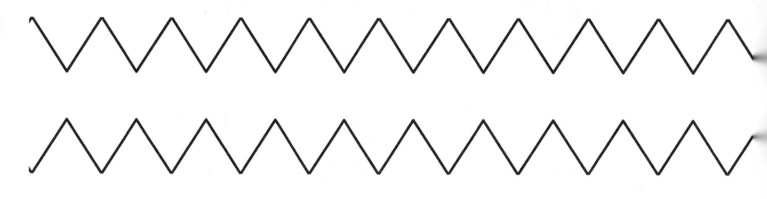

```
A T A Y E R H O L H L Y
E F H K A L B W T D I M
R S Q N A T I O N J G U
F D T T V R H G E E A H
D R C O R Q A I R N S I
K U U M B A Y M Z T E N
A M V T F I O D U E S D
L S E P U M P K I N U I
A J B E N D E R A A Q N
I R Q V I N A C I S E J
E H I S T O R Y J Y I E
W D H A Y T E N F S N F
```

Let's solve the maze. Good luck!

Write the missing letters in the blank spaces so that they form the correct word.

1. | B | | | D | | | A |

2. | K | | | | B | |

3. | U | | I | | Y |

   | C | | |

4. | U | | I | | A |

Color them all!

Trace the lines.

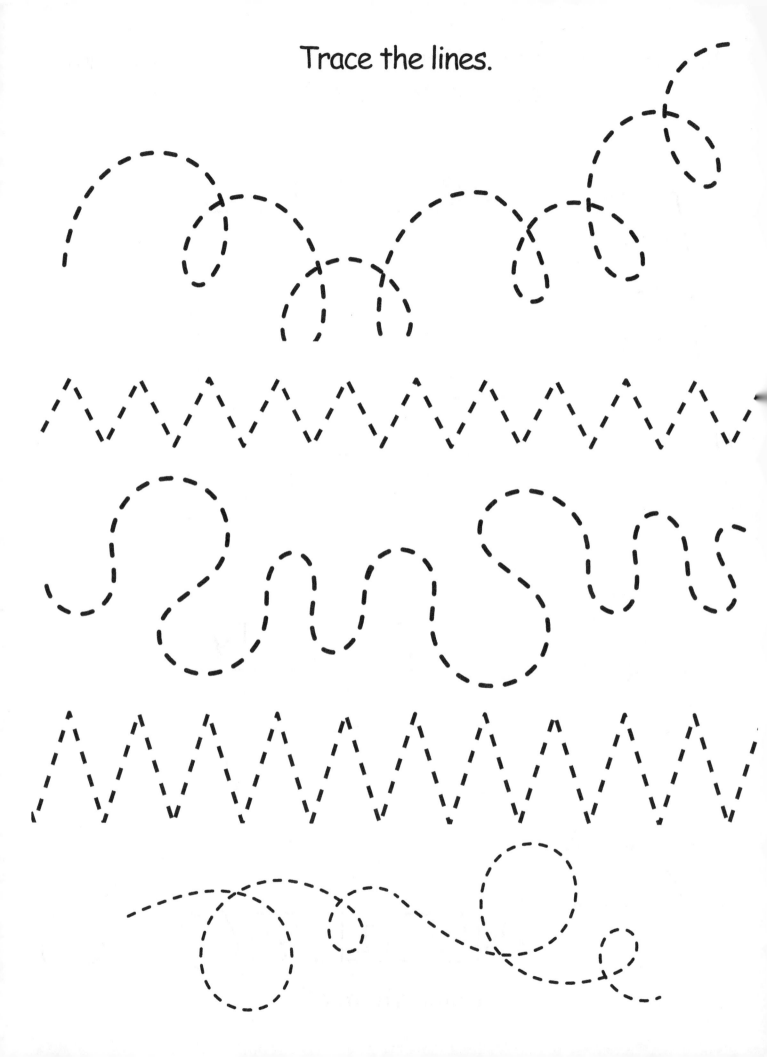

KARAMU

(kah-RAH-moo)

Karamu is a festival that falls on the sixth day of Kwanzaa,
the day of the Kuumba principle.
Families get together with their relatives and friends,
have dinner together and afterwards dance, sing
and tell each other stories.

Find 5 differences between the pictures.

Color them all!

Find 9 words related to Kwanzaa.
Search words in directions:

```
A R D Y E R H O L H F Y
N F U J A M A W T D A T
C S Q M P E R H S P I L
E H R C O M M U N I T Y
S E A O R J W E E N H N
T I M R O W A A Z E Y T
O P G K F I Z A W A D I
R S O X E A E I T P U B
S B L E S K I N G P Q A
K U J I C H A G U L I A
E B S A L G V L D E I F
W D H R E S P E C T N I
```

- Umoja
- Faith
- Kujichagulia
- Ujama
- Mkeka
- Ancestors
- Zawadi
- Community
- Pineapple

See the solution on the next page :)

```
A R D Y E R H O L H F Y
N F U J A M A W T D A T
C S Q M P E R H S P I L
E H R C O M M U N I T Y
S E A O R J W E E N H N
T I M R O W A A Z E Y T
O P G K F I Z A W A D I
R S O X E A E I T P U B
S B L E S K I N G P Q A
K U J I C H A G U L I A
E B S A L G V L D E I F
W D H R E S P E C T N I
```

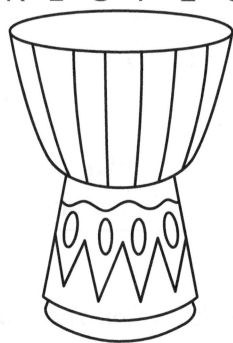

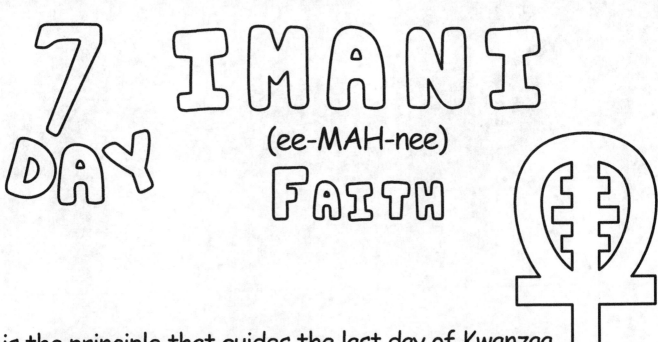

7 DAY IMANI
(ee-MAH-nee)
FAITH

It is the principle that guides the last day of Kwanzaa.
This means believing wholeheartedly in ourselves,
our family, our leaders and winning our struggles.
On the seventh day we light the last green candle.

Count all the items and write the answer in the empty
Circles at the bottom of the page.

Color them all!

Let's solve the maze. Good luck!

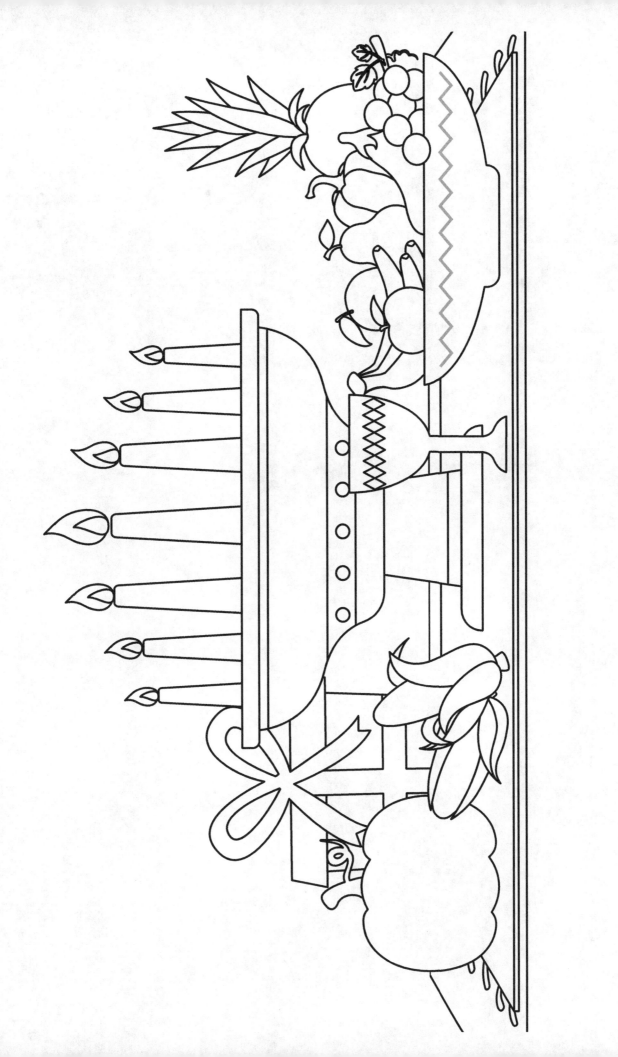

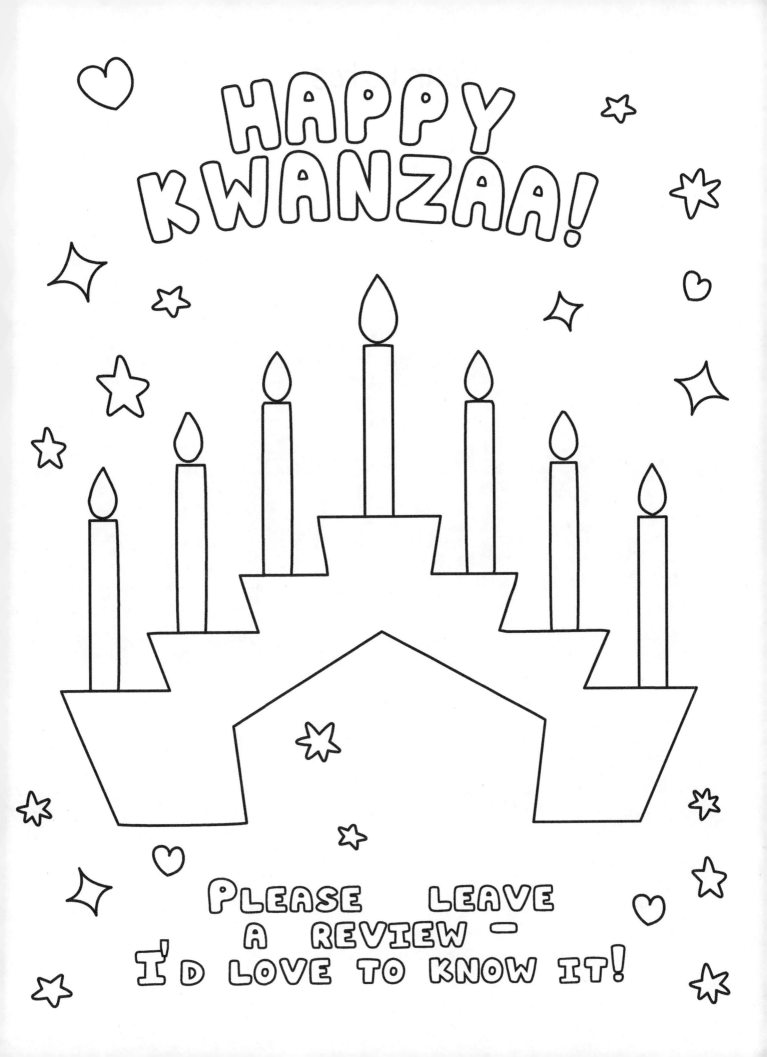

Your notes

Your notes

Your notes